Animal Professions

Interesting Facts about Animals for Children and Parents

derived from various sources. Please consult a licensed professional before attempting any techniques outlined in this book.

By reading this document, the reader agrees that under no circumstances is the author responsible for any losses, direct or indirect, that are incurred as a result of the use of information contained within this document, including, but not limited to, errors, omissions, or inaccuracies.

Table of Contents

Introduction

Animals are everywhere. We see them every day, and sometimes we see them so often that we don't pay them much attention. Others, we pay a lot of attention to, and some we might even be afraid of.

Nobody wants to get sprayed by a skunk! Eww, the smell! And do you scream when you see a mouse or a rat? How about when an opossum stares down at you from a tree? Does your Mom or Dad get mad when a squirrel eats all of the seed they put out for the birds?

We all react to animals differently, but did you know that each animal has a special job to do? They each have a profession, just like our moms and dads, teachers, police officers, utility workers and everyone who has a job.

Let's look at some of the professions animals have.

Chapter 1: Domestic Animals

Domestic animals are those we have as pets. They are domesticated by humans so that they are tame, and they depend on us for survival. They don't live in the wild, and they don't have to hunt for their food. A domestic animal is simply known as a pet.

Some animals can be either wild or domestic, such as rats. Some people have pet rats that they care for in cages. Other rats live in the wild, usually along riverbanks. We'll learn more about rats later, but for now, our domestic animals will introduce themselves.

Dogs

Hi, I'm a dog. I am known as 'Man's Best Friend'. Sometimes, people will bring me home when I'm just a puppy, and sometimes I'm an adult when they take me in.

I can be really small, so small that you can fit me in your coat pocket, or I can be really big, even bigger than a person! No matter what my size, I am loyal. I will protect my owners, and I will bark to warn them of danger.

Some of my canine friends work as service dogs. That means they help people get where they need to go. Some of my buddies work with children who have health problems. We have many jobs, and we love to give love and get it in return.

Cats

How do you do? I am a cat. When I'm young, I'm called a kitten. I love living with humans, especially those who like to cuddle with me.

There are so many different breeds, but being different on the outside doesn't make us different on the inside. Do you know my purring helps humans to sleep, and some scientists say it can help with heart and muscle health? That's right; I am a great pet to have for good health. I guess you could say I'm a doctor!

Horses

Howdy! I am a horse. I usually live in a stable, and my owner will let me roam in a fenced-in meadow or pasture. I come in different breeds. Some horses are big and strong and can be hooked to special equipment to plow a field for planting. Other horses pull sleighs so that people can have a nice ride. Before there were cars, people had to ride horses to get to where they needed to go. We were the primary source of transportation.

We have many jobs, and we love to run free and play. A fun fact about us is that we're measured in 'hands.' A hand is equal to four inches. We like to swim too! We are like teachers because we teach humans patience and trust

Chapter 2: Farm Animals

If you've ever visited a farm, or taken a ride in the country, you've most likely seen a farm animal. Talk about being busy! Farm animals have many important responsibilities. Without farm animals, you would have no milk to drink or wool for blankets and sweaters.

We have some farm animals waiting to meet you!

Cows

Moo! How are you? I am a cow, and I'd like you to meet my friends and relatives. We do different jobs, so we have different names. Some of us were given our names because of where we were born and raised. Some of us live in the United States and Canada and some of us live in Britain.

Some of us give you the milk you drink every day. From that milk you can make cheese and yogurt and many other yummy things to eat. We provide humans with meat and our fur makes nice, warm rugs.

Baby cows are called calves, and big, strong male cows are called bulls. Sometimes, the big, strong cows and bulls can be harnessed and plow fields just like horses! We have many different jobs, and we try to do each one well.

Goat

Hi there! I'm a goat, and you can usually find me on a farm, grazing on grass or anything edible, even cardboard, but I don't like meat or milk. The funny thing is that we goats produce milk that humans like. Our milk is used to make soaps and cheeses too.

Humans love to shave us and use our fur to make yarn. It is warm and cozy.

We aren't always in a good mood, so you don't want to pet us without an adult with you. We can kick and bite, so never come near us when you are alone. We don't mean to hurt anyone, but sometimes it happens.

Our work is to make life better for humans by providing nice products and good milk.

Sheep

Baaaa! We are happy you want to learn a little about us. We are called lambs when we are babies and when we are all grown up, we're called sheep.

We produce the wool that's used to make a lot of clothing. Our fur coat is sheared once or twice a year. It's just like when you get a haircut! Once our wool is removed, it gets cleaned and processed and sold to people who make it into yarn. Sometimes, it's used for stuffing pillows and dolls. Our job is to make sure there's enough wool to make all of the things that humans depend on.

Female sheep produce milk, and people love it. Do you know another name for a female sheep? It's ewe! Pronounced the same as the word 'you'. I love ewe!

Pigs

Oink, oink! We are pigs, and our babies are called piglets. We love living on farms and rolling in the mud.

We have many uses. Our meat is used for people to eat, and our bristly hairs are used to make brushes.

We have such a good sense of smell, and we are often used to hunt for truffles, a delicacy found in France and England. A delicacy is a food that's not easily found that humans like to eat. I guess you could call us treasure hunters!

We are usually pink or white, and some of us are black or spotted, and we grow really big! Not all of us are nice, and we do bite, so be careful around us.

Llamas

Hi! I am a llama. Do you like my silly name? You might think I look silly too, but I can be your best friend. I make a good companion for anyone who wants a dependable, trustworthy friend.

My wool is used to make yarn, and, boy, does it make soft yarn. I don't just hang around all day and do nothing, I am a good guardian. I can protect sheep and goats and other livestock from predators.

I guess you could say I'm a superhero! I won't let anything get too close to those I guard and protect.

Farm Dogs

Hello. I'm a Border Collie. Border Collie is a breed of dog that is great at working on a farm. We Border Collies are very athletic, and we are highly intelligent.

We are best known for our ability to herd sheep, and cows too! If we aren't used for herding, we make great family pets, but if we are used for herding, we should not be around children without adult supervision. We are smart, and if we see children running, we might try to herd them too!

Chapter 3: Rodents

The rodent family includes mice, rats, chipmunks, and squirrels. Surprisingly, at one time, rabbits were in the rodent family, but they are no longer.

Some of us think of rodents as icky and some people are scared to see a tiny mouse run across a room. They might jump on a chair or run away from it.

The rodent family is eager to meet you, so let's get right to it!

Mice

Hello! I am a mouse. When there are more than one of us, we are called mice. We are very important to the cycle of life. We like to eat a lot. We might be tiny, but we can eat 15-20 times in a day. We aren't fussy. We'll eat most anything that is around.

We can play dead, and some of us can jump really high. When we run, we run in a zigzag motion, but we sure are fast. Some humans are really afraid of us, but we are really more afraid of them.

Rats

Hi-de-ho! I'm a rat, a member of the rodent family. You might think of me as a pest, but do you know I'm really good at trash removal? That's right! I will roam the streets and eat garbage. I help to keep the streets free of debris. Sure, I've been known to dumpster dive, but that's only if I can't find anything on the street.

I have an excellent memory, and I never get lost. I only need to travel to a destination once to be able to find my way back. Some people keep rats as pets. Those who do get to live in cages in a warm house. We make nice pets for humans who aren't afraid of us.

Chipmunks

Hi! I'm a chipmunk. I love to eat nuts, and I store them in my cheeks. I like walking on walls, and just hanging around.

Some people say I'm a nuisance, but I don't do damage on purpose. I do help by eating insects that humans don't like and that cause damage or can cause sickness.

I don't carry any illnesses, and I am not harmful to humans.

Squirrels

Thanks for stopping by! Your mom and dad might think I am a bother, but they might not realize that I am like an arborist. My family, friends, and I work hard to gather seeds and spread some of them so that new trees and vegetation can grow.

I have a very large family and circle of friends. You've probably seen some of us running in your yard or in the street. You might have seen us playing in trees. We do like to play!

Marmots

Howdy! We marmots are just large versions of squirrels. I think we look like something between a squirrel and a beaver.

We marmots are good at watching for predators, and when we spot one, plug your ears because we can be loud! You might not have ever seen one of us because we aren't found in the United States or Canada. We live all around Asia and the Himalayas.

Meerkats

Hello! I am a meerkat, and I am native to South Africa. I usually hang with my family as we like to stay in groups. We are good at being watch guards, and we don't like birds or airplanes.

I can stand for a long time without getting tired. That's why meerkats are so good at guarding. We like to play, and we like to chase. We live far underground in burrows. Sometimes we move around a lot. We like our burrows to be cool, especially when it's hot outside.

You won't see a meerkat unless you're in South Africa, but you can find a lot of pictures of us online. Yes, we do take selfies!

Beavers

Hi friends! I'm a beaver. I'm the second largest rodent in the world! I build dams and canals. I'm nocturnal, so you might not see me too often. Nocturnal means I'm more active at night. I kind of like the nightlife because it's quieter, and much easier to cross the road because there's less traffic.
I am always busy building. It's my favorite thing to do!

Chapter 4: Other Animals

There are other animals that fall into various categories. Let's explore some of them. You're sure to find some are familiar and some are not so familiar.

Rabbits

Hoppity hello! We are rabbits, and we can run fast and we love to hop. You might catch us in your garden munching on your vegetables, but did you know that we also fertilize the grass and your garden? Our waste products make a great fertilizer.

Some of us have angora hair that is spun into beautiful, soft yarns. We make great pets too, but you can't capture us from outside. To have a rabbit for a pet, you need to buy one from a breeder.

Opossums

Greetings! I am an opossum, not to be confused with my cousin, the possum. I like to hang out in trees, but you might see me scurrying around the ground. That's because I love to eat ticks, and the more ticks I eat, the safer it is for humans. Ticks carry diseases, and I don't want my human friends to get sick, so my friends and I eat as many ticks each day as possible. We are tick eradicators!

Skunks

Hey, please don't plug your nose! I know, I know. I have a bad reputation for being stinky, and I sure can be smelly, but that's only when I am defending myself.

I am not as bad as most humans think. I eat lots of insects. That includes insects that hurt people and make them sick.

Moles

Hello! I can't see you too well because I have poor eyesight, but I'm not blind. I know I'm not the best looking animal you've seen, but I am kind of cute.

I love to dig tunnels and I eat a lot of insects and worms. You might not see me too often, or maybe never at all, because I live underground most of the time. I'm sort of like a coal miner, walking through tunnels and spending a lot of time underground.

Otters

Hi! I am an otter. I live near water, and I love to swim. I can be a sound sleeper, so when I sleep in the water, I grab hold of seaweed so I don't float away!

I am a social animal, and I like to hunt for shellfish. I only weigh about 30 pounds, but you should see me crack a shellfish open with my stomach!

Conclusion

We hope you enjoyed meeting all of the different animals and learning about them. Whether they are domestic or wild, animals make a great contribution to our ecosystem and to humankind.

We need animals not only for human survival, but for the survival of earth. Whether an animal is providing comfort to a child or dropping seeds that give us more vegetation, every animal has a purpose.

You might have a cat or a dog, or even a rabbit. If you do have a pet, then you know its importance to you. A pet can bring us great comfort and companionship. Animals that live in the wild can be fun to watch, and amazing too! Have you ever watched a busy squirrel prepare for winter? They can carry a lot of sticks and grass in their mouths.

We hope you'll be observant of the animals around you, and watch their habits. Not only is it fun, but it's educational. From all of our featured animals, we say thank you and it was a pleasure to meet you!